FRUIT OF THE SPIRIT

PEACE

Fruit of the Spirit Study Guide Series

Love

Joy

Peace

Patience

Kindness

Goodness

Faithfulness

Gentleness

Self-Control

CALVIN MILLER

 FRUIT OF THE SPIRIT

PEACE

Published in Nashville, Tennessee, by Thomas Nelson. Thomas Nelson is a trademark of Thomas Nelson, Inc.

Typesetting by Gregory C. Benoit Publishing, Old Mystic, CT GCB

Thomas Nelson, Inc., titles may be purchased in bulk for educational, business, fund-raising, or sales promotional use. For information, please e-mail SpecialMarkets@ThomasNelson.com.

ISBN: 978-1-4185-2838-6

Printed in the United States of America
08 09 10 11 12 RRD 9 8 7 6 5 4 3 2 1

TABLE OF CONTENTS

But the fruit of the Spirit is love, joy, peace, patience, kind-
ness, goodness, faithfulness, gentleness and self-control.
Against such things there is no law.
—Galatians 5:22–23

INTRODUCTION

Peace isn't something we obtain; it is something we become as God's Spirit gains control of our lives. Only by God's Spirit can a person face life's uncertainties with a calm assurance that God is in control. Maybe you've been there. Maybe you need to be there.

This study is about peace as a fruit of the Spirit. We'll discover what it means to be at peace with God and then to embody the peace of God. The latter is dependent upon the former. Authentic peace is a natural by-product of a believer's relationship with God. Where there is no peace, there is a flaw in that relationship.

Throughout the Bible, God's peace comforted people whose lives were in turmoil. Like a thick fog rolling through a valley, God's peace can overwhelm us so that we see God rather than our circumstances. God's peace isn't the absence of strife but rather the presence of God in the midst of our strife.

Paul understood tension. He had to run for his life several times. He spent time in prison. He was beaten and even shipwrecked. Yet through it all, he was at peace. How? That's what this study is all about. As you work through the pages that follow, you will see peace as something to be accessed, not acquired.

When we accept God's offer of salvation, we allow his Spirit to move into our lives. With that Spirit comes God's characteristics—one of those characteristics being peace. So, God's peace is deposited into the lives of believers. We must simply make withdrawals from the "bank." We make a terrible mistake when we attempt to obtain peace through any other means.

Over the next six weeks, you will be given the opportunity to let God's peace flood your life. When Paul listed peace as one of the fruits of the Spirit, he identified it as a characteristic of God that, when reflected to the world around us, draws people to him.

Have you ever met a person who was overwhelmed with God's peace? Someone who, no matter what life delivers, takes it in stride knowing that God knew well in advance what would happen? That is the peace of God that comes to us as we give him more and more control of our lives. It is hard to lay our concerns at the foot of the Cross, but it is something we must continually do. Jesus gives us peace; will you accept his gift?

HOW TO USE THIS GUIDE

Galatians 5:22–23 is not a plan to achieve better faith. Rather, it is a description of God's personal gifts to all of us. If we follow God and seek his blessing, then the fruits of the Spirit are a natural overflow in our relationship with God. We are to grow in character so that one day we will reflect the image of our Lord.

This series of nine six-week studies will clearly focus your spiritual life to become more like Christ. Each study guide is divided into six weeks, and each of the six-week courses covers one of the fruits of the Spirit. Participants simply read each daily study and answer the questions at the end of each devotional. This prepares everyone for the group discussion at the end of the week.

Each week features a similar pattern that explores one aspect of that study's fruit of the Spirit. The first lesson establishes the aspect of the fruit to be explored throughout the week. The second lesson looks at the week's theme as it relates to God's purpose in the life of the believer. The third lesson looks at the week's theme as it relates to the believer's relationship with Christ. The fourth lesson explores how the fruit is relevant in service to others. And in the fifth lesson, the theme is related to personal worship. A sixth lesson is included as a bonus study, and focuses on either a biblical character who modeled this particular fruit, or a key parable that brings the theme into focus.

Each weeklong study should conclude in a group review. The weekly group discussion serves as a place to understand the practical side of the theme and receive encouragement and feedback on the journey to become more Christlike. For the study to have the character-transforming effect God desires, it is important for the participant to spend ten to twenty minutes a day reading the Scripture passage and the devotional, and to think through the two questions for the day. If each participant reads all of the questions beforehand, it greatly enhances the group dynamic. Each participant should choose three or four questions to discuss during the group session.

These simple guidelines will help make group time productive. Take a total of about forty-five minutes to answer and discuss the questions. Each person need not answer every question, but be sure all members participate. You can stimulate participation by having everyone respond to an icebreaker question. Have each group member answer the first of the six questions listed at the end of the week, and leave the remaining questions open-ended. Or, make up your own icebreaker question, such as: What color best represents the day you are having? What is your favorite movie? Or, how old were you when you had your first kiss?

No one should respond to all of the questions. Keep in mind that if you are always talking, the others are not. It is essential that everyone contribute. If you notice that someone is not participating, ask that group member which question is the most relevant. Be sensitive if something is keeping that member from contributing. Don't ask someone to read or pray aloud unless you know that the member is comfortable with such a task.

Always start and end your time with prayer. Sometimes it helps to have each person say what he or she plans to do with the lesson that week. Remember to reserve ten minutes for group prayer. You might want to keep a list of requests and answers to prayer at the back of this book.

Week 1: Peace—A Truce with God

Memory Passage for the Week: John 14:27

Day 1: Peace—A Truce with God

We can rest peacefully in the knowledge that when God establishes his covenants, they are forever through all time. Genesis 9:8–17.

Day 2: The Purpose of God in My Life

Peace is not something we create within ourselves and then extend to God. Peace is rooted and nourished in the very soil of his mercy. Titus 3:3–11.

Day 3: My Relationship with Christ

The human heart is subject to turmoil, but Jesus enters our hearts to save us, and a calm falls over all our turmoil like oil falls on water. Colossians 3:15.

Day 4: My Service to Others

Christians ought to frame a benediction of peace and hang the phrase in the gallery of their hearts. Numbers 6:22–26.

Day 5: My Personal Worship

God's peace results in a new freedom that makes a home in our worship. When we worship the Prince of Peace, his peace will sustain us. Romans 16:20.

Day 6: A Character Study on Samuel

1 Samuel 8:1–22

Day 7: Group Discussion

Day 1: Peace—A Truce with God

Read Genesis 9:8–17

There is no way to understand Genesis 9, the story of God's covenant with Noah, without first understanding Genesis 6:5–9, the story of the Flood. It grieved God that the human beings he had created had fallen, and everything in their imaginations was continually evil. In Genesis 6, God resolved to wipe humankind from the planet.

In the next three chapters God sent Noah to build an ark, and he then sent a great flood to wipe away all the sinful people from the face of the earth. When the flood was finished, God called a truce with earth. The idea of any further universal judgment by flood was concluded with a promise and a sign. The promise was "never again" (Genesis 9:11), and the sign was a rainbow (v. 13).

The truce God secured with Noah and his children was finalized by the very powerful words: "never again," and "for all generations to come" (v.12). When God establishes his covenants, they are forever.

One wonders if this promise of God was not rooted in the pain of watching his creatures drowning in the deluge as it wiped out all life. But perhaps there was a certain awe in the eyes of Noah and his family as they sailed alone upon a vast sea of death—a water-world with no hint of land!

God offered a truce—a covenant—just so they knew they would never have to live in terror ever again. With such a promise Noah and his family could leave their boat on Mount Ararat and live in bright security for the rest of their lives.

But these same words, "never again" and "for all generations," also pertain to the Christian life. Jesus died and ended our estrangement from God. Never again do we need to fear that Christ will abandon us. The cross, like the rainbow, is God's seal and image of peace.

We who believe in Christ are kept by God's promise of "never again." Christ has died. There is a grand rainbow of promise arching over all our insecurities. Hell is simply not an option for all those who look at the cross and cry, "*Credo* ... I believe."

Questions for Personal Reflection

1. Have you experienced a truce with God? If so, how? If not, why?

2. How can you help others experience a truce with God?

Day 2: The Purpose of God in My Life
Read Titus 3:3–11

This passage in Titus describes the peaceless lives many of us live or have once lived: lives of foolishness and disobedience when we were deceived by all kinds of passions and pleasures; lives of hopelessness, envy, and malice (Titus 3:3). That is, until into our turmoil walked the peace of Christ. God saved us by sending his Son (v. 5), and the Holy Spirit raised a white flag over all our turmoil. We were called to peace.

Through Christ we learn that our contrition is less contentious, our bitterness is less harsh, and our troubled spirits can hear the words "peace, be still"—if we just listen. Can you remember where his "peace, be still" found you? Has it found you? The storms of meaninglessness rage all about us. The winds of indecision buffet us. The tides of turmoil rage. We know not who we are. We find no pier of support in all the turbulence, until Christ comes with his "peace, be still."

Christ's peace counsels those who love divisive behavior to put their quarrelsome nature aside and enjoy the quiet. He inspires Christians who once loved argument to avoid controversy and despise foolish quarrels (vv. 9–11).

So peace and making peace is a purpose of God in our lives. When we come upon God's grace, which saves us not because of righteous things we do but because of his mercy, and we receive his peace, then we can publish his grace and others may discover his salvation. Then those who are newly born again know it is never because of right things they have done but because of his mercy that his peace became theirs. God's salvation is free and his peace is for all.

Questions for Personal Reflection

1. What robs us of our peace?

2. In what situations do you need to make peace with God and with others?

Day 3: My Relationship with Christ

Read Colossians 3:15

The glorious thing about peace is that it is the soul of our relationship with Christ. We relate to Christ; we converse with Christ; we experience and grow in him only when his peace is the very atmosphere that shelters our ongoing relationship with him. The word *rule* in Colossians 3:15 really means to "umpire" or "arbitrate" the struggles and disquietudes of our lives.

Richard Dawkins, a prominent twentieth-century scientist and philosopher, rejected traditional Christianity because he felt its fierce doctrinal nature inspired quarrels over truth that divided the Christian world into angry denominations. He said Christian doctrine spawned bloodshed, ethnic cleansing, wars, and crusades. One cannot disagree that much of the history of the church has been that of quarreling Christians championing viewpoints rather than celebrating their great commonalities in peace. But the apostle Paul suggested that each Christian needs to let the peace of Christ arbitrate in his or her own soul. Then when the peace of Christ rules the inner life of the individual, perhaps it will rule in the church universal.

We must be honest even when it hurts. Disputes over doctrines have often brought about the fiercest of separations in our Christianity. Individual viewpoints push Christians into provinces of tiny differences, small-walled kingdoms of hot debate. And why? If Christ rules from the throne of our hearts, surely we can trust each other to love all those he loves.

Martyrs die for Christ; they do not die for viewpoints. Yet sometimes Christian power-mongers kill other Christians who do not believe the same things about Christ that they do. It is an odd obscenity that some Christians would kill other Christians in the name of Christ. Wouldn't it be wonderful if all Christians could abandon their hatred? Wouldn't it be nice if everybody could just *live* for Jesus?

Questions for Personal Reflection

1. Are you more passionate about your relationship with God or your viewpoint on certain issues?

2. What is the danger of focusing on issues more than on God's love?

Day 4: My Service to Others

Read Romans 6:22–26

How are we to serve others in the ministry of peace? Aaron taught the Israelites to bless each other with a benediction of peace. Benedictions of peace help each of us minister to others by seeking for them a life free of turmoil. It is godly to bless the turbulence out of our turmoil. When we help others discover the indwelling of Christ, we bring his peace to a troubled world.

A life without peace is hell. By publishing peace, it is possible to help take the hell out of the right now. If hell were only out there in the future, people would scarcely give it a thought. But hell is now. Hell is here. Hell is divorce, pain, cancer, family dysfunction, and job loss. Hell is neurosis, addiction, codependency, and grief. To all these struggles we offer our benediction.

One prominent American clergyman tells in one of his sermons about a Christmas Eve when his father gave a dollar (quite a sum in the early part of the twentieth century) to a homeless person. "I give you this in the name of Christ," said the father. "Thank you," said the homeless man. "I accept this in the name of Christ."

What wonders are wrought when we say, "The Lord bless you and keep you, the Lord make his face to shine upon you and be gracious unto you, the Lord turn his face toward you and give you peace."

Questions for Personal Reflection

1. How do you experience the peace of God in your daily life?

2. How can you help others experience God's peace?

Day 5: My Personal Worship
Read Romans 16:20

God's grace is to afford those who long to praise him an atmosphere free of spiritual struggle. Satan is the author of all such struggles, so Paul makes it clear that God is going to crush Satan under the heel of those who become spiritually powerful by serving their appetite for God.

Once Satan is driven from life, the turmoil will be gone, and we can praise God in perfect peace. Nothing is more beautiful than to exalt God and achieve in Christ an inner atmosphere free of all turmoil. After Jesus was victorious over Satan in the wilderness, angels ministered to him. After the reign of Satan is over in our own lives, peace will be born and adoration will erupt in joy.

Alienation is always sponsored by evil. Just as God draws us to himself, Satan drives wedges into that holy relationship. Satan actively works at trying to limit the number of God's friends.

The God of peace will crush Satan under his feet. What a great promise this is. All of our lives Satan has kept us in turmoil. He has agitated our troubled minds with hatred, self-will, and ambition. He has left us weeping in despair, helpless before our hopelessness. Satan is the author of our identity crisis, the breaker of our hope. He always comes shod in the muddy boots that stomp our desire for clean morality into unwholesome pleasures.

But Jesus reigns! Our old enemy is crushed. Hallelujah!

Questions for Personal Reflection

1. How can you renew your peace each day?

2. How might the world view your peace?

Day 6: Samuel—A Peaceful Resolution
Read 1 Samuel 8:1–22

Samuel, in his old age, was a prophet scarred by conflicts. First of all, things were not working out well in his family life. He had two sons, Joel and Abijah (*Abiah* in some Scripture versions), whom he appointed as judges in Israel. Alas, his sons did not "walk in his ways" (1 Samuel 8:3). They accepted bribes and were continually involved in dishonest dealings.

Second, Samuel was at an impasse with the nation of Israel as to what kind of government they should have. His countrymen wanted him to end the judgeships that had a four-century history in Israel. Israel wanted a king. Samuel reminded them that a king would levy a military draft and a taxation system. Things would become repressive and unbearable under a monarchy:

> *This is what the king who will reign over you will do: He will take your sons and make them serve with his chariots and horses, and they will run in front of his chariots ... He will take your daughters to be perfumers and cooks and bakers. He will take the best of your fields and vineyards and olive groves and give them to his attendants. He will take a tenth of your grain and of your vintage and give it to his officials and attendants. Your menservants and maidservants and the*

best of your cattle and donkeys he will take for his own use.
He will take a tenth of your flocks, and you yourselves will
become his slaves. When that day comes, you will cry out
for relief from the king you have chosen, and the LORD will
not answer you in that day.

—1 Samuel 8:11–18

The Israelites did not accept Samuel's logic and went on clamoring for a king. Samuel became a person in deep turmoil. Finally the Lord resolved these differences. The Lord counseled Samuel, "Listen to them and give them a king" (v. 22).

God spoke.

The decision was made.

Following the decision came peace. Peace always follows the resolution of conflict. Conflicts are nearly all resolved when we decide that God has spoken and we obey. It is difficult to tell if Samuel wholly agreed with God in this matter, but he did obey. Obedience results in peace. Rebellion is the parent of turmoil.

It is in this context that Samuel learned the beauty of conflict resolution. Peace, however, is always more than just the cessation of a quarrel. Peace is a single focus. Look at two things long enough, and your eyes will cross and your mind will splinter. Look at one thing only, and that single focus will bring peace.

Samuel at first tried to focus on both God's command and his desire for Israel. When he narrowed his focus to God's commands, peace was his at once.

Questions for Personal Reflection

1. Is it more important to you that you win a quarrel or that you achieve peace?

Why?

2. When have you experienced the peace that results from obedience to God?

Day 7: Group Discussion

The following questions should take about forty-five minutes to answer and discuss. Each member should answer the first question, leaving the remaining questions open-ended. Everyone need not answer, but be sure all members participate.

1. *When peace is absent, some would argue that God is absent. Do you agree with this line of thinking? Why or why not?*

2. *What does it mean to be at peace with God?*

3.   *Why is it so common for us to live such peaceless lives?*

4.   *How can we become one with other believers? What are the things that stand in our way?*

5.   *What demons of peacelessness need to be driven from our lives? How can we drive away these demons?*

6.   *What is the role of our fellowship with other believers in protecting us from Satan's attempts to rob us of our peace?*

Week 2: The Prince of Peace

Memory Passage for the Week: Isaiah 26:3

Day 1: The Prince of Peace

Jesus won our peace for us when he died on the cross. We never need to fear that our sins will bar us from his eternal peace. Genesis 14:17–20

Day 2: The Purpose of God in My Life

God has ordained that each of us become peacemakers who sow peace and produce a harvest of righteousness. James 3:18.

Day 3: My Relationship with Christ

Christ mediates our needs, cleansing turbulence from our lives and giving us quality. Hebrews 7:1–3.

Day 4: My Service to Others

We are to live so much in the center of Christ's peace that we may exude that same peace, and as a result it becomes to those around us a haven from their own turbulence. 2 Peter 3:14.

Day 5: My Personal Worship

Our quiet time in the presence of the Savior ought to be approached, enjoyed, and left on a note of quiet and untroubled love. Proverbs 12:20.

Day 6: A Character Study on Hezekiah

2 Kings 18:1–5

Day 7: Group Discussion

Day 1: The Prince of Peace

Read Genesis 14:17–20

The cryptic king of Salem, Melchizedek, holds for many a spellbinding sense of mystery. He was intriguing because of who he was and what he meant. Melchizedek, whose name means "the king of peace," appeared suddenly to bless Abram and then just as suddenly disappeared. The mystery of his priesthood, dedicated to the God Most High is a sort of archetype of Christ.

Jesus, like Melchizedek, became a high priest forever—not on the basis of his ancestry but on the "basis of the power of an indestructible life" (Hebrews 7:16). One of the functions of a priest is intercession. According to this passage as well as Romans 8:34, Jesus is our High Priest, always living and ever interceding for us.

Jesus the Priest—the constantly interceding priest—is our hope. He continues interceding when we think we've grown too busy to pray. Always at his post, Jesus prays for us. Life becomes manageable—not always because we have been faithful but because Jesus is our priest forever in the order of Melchizedek.

Have you any turmoil in your life? Let it go. Are you afraid that your personality is so flawed that God might never really accept you? Rejoice! You have a continually interceding priest, Jesus Christ the Righteous.

Christ won our peace on a bloody hill. And even as he died he secured our right to immediate access to the Father. Best of all, his sacrifice was sufficient enough that we never need fear that any of our sins will prevent our entrance to heaven, nor can our moral weaknesses bar us from his eternal peace.

Questions for Personal Reflection

1. What keeps you from praying?

2. How do you feel knowing that Jesus intercedes on your behalf?

Day 2: The Purpose of God in My Life
James 3:18

How do we become peacemakers who sow peace and reap a harvest of righteousness? One of the most exciting parts of our lives in Christ is that we are called to evangelize with ministries of peace. The world is a troubled place. Most people have never known God's prescription for peace. Jesus is that prescription, and we are the apothecaries of peace.

James says we are to be peacemakers who sow in peace. In this he sounds like his brother according to the flesh, Jesus, who taught in the Beatitudes: "Blessed are the peacemakers" (Matthew 5:9). The church in every generation is hungry for people who are called to make peace. Evangelists are always to be publishers of peace. But beyond the roles of evangelism, there are enough "individual differences" in all congregations to blow them apart if we allow these differences to exist without being moderated by those who are called to peace.

Many atheist philosophers have looked at quarreling churches and decided that, even in their own peacelessness, they could not risk serving a Christ who, in their minds, created such a warlike faith.

The church—how pitiably true—always seems to be a hangout for grudges. In the book of Philippians, Paul confronted two quarreling sisters, Euodia and Syntyche, to bring their clashing spirits into calm, and he asked for whomever received the letter to play the role of peacemaker in adjudicating the quarrel (Philippians 4:2). This passage should remind us that the church in every age is well served by those who pray for and are able to bless their disagreeing members back into harmony.

Questions for Personal Reflection

1. What is the ultimate purpose of a peacemaker?

2. How can you become a peacemaker?

Day 3: My Relationship with Christ

Read Hebrews 7:1–3

Is your heart a prayer room? Visualize your heart as the place you meet with Christ. I have written on this very metaphor in a book called *The Table of Inwardness*. In this small book I pictured myself in concord with Jesus, sitting at a table set for two. The setting of my prayer rendezvous with Christ is always a garden of peace.

If there are things in my life that bring turmoil to the setting, I ask Jesus to clear away the busy noise of my self-important agenda so we can meet in peace. But how do we get rid of that busy inner noise that produces restlessness in our hearts? This is indeed difficult. All of our lives, from the time we are first able to think, we talk to ourselves inside our minds. We live all our lives in this never-ending stream of conversation. Our minds are chatty, never stopping to rest. We talk, talk, talk inside ourselves. Unfortunately, "inside ourselves" is the only address we can give to God. Here in our mental chatter lives the Holy Spirit, always trying to get a word in edgewise.

This unending stream of mental commentary that each of us hears as we walk through life needs to come to a halt if we are to hear the word of Christ over our inner, mental roar. I suggest that we practice a discipline called *centering*, in which we focus on something, or someone—like Christ himself—until we call the noise to silence. Then we can press on to learn the art of listening prayer.

It is then that peace will be born in our lives. With this new calm, Christ is ours. He is ours for fellowship and ours for instruction. He is ours for friendship and commission. He is ours for the moderated life; ours for the life of peace.

Questions for Personal Reflection

1. How can you make your quiet times with God more important?

2. Why is it important to spend time listening when praying?

Day 4: My Service to Others
Read 2 Peter 3:14

Peter encourages us to make every effort to be "spotless, blameless and at peace" (2 Peter 3:14). How would such a personal resolve improve our service to others? Such a resolution, if carried out, would keep us open to whatever ministry God calls us to perform.

Christians who live in inner turmoil do not attract converts. Our own private battles usually keep us from seeing those around us who may be in even greater need. Indeed we must call these inner wars to peace before we can serve to our fullest potential either Christ or our world.

The truth is that people who are at peace make excellent ministers. The world is unafraid of peacemakers. Peacemakers have no desire to use other people to arrive at some agenda of their own. Peacemakers exist to create an attitude, a mood, and an atmosphere that makes other people unafraid.

In fact, the very appearance of a peacemaker seems to say, "Be not afraid ... take a load off your anxieties ... let's sit down and talk together." It is much like the appearance of angels in the Scripture. Take, for instance, their appearance to the frightened shepherds in Luke's nativity account. The angels cried, "Fear not" (Luke 2:10 KJV). It was probably a bit too late, for seeing an angel would tend to cause a strong reaction. But the message of the angels was a message of profound peace.

If there is any real ministry that brings joy to God, it must be to give the terrified a little security. Nothing is worse than fear. But we who love Christ are to enter our world of frightened souls announcing Christ's message of peace.

Questions for Personal Reflection

1. What are the places in which you can announce God's peace?

2. Who are the people who are in most need of God's peace?

Day 5: My Personal Worship
Read Proverbs 12:20

There is indeed "deceit in the hearts of those who plot evil," but there is "joy for those who promote peace" (Proverbs 12:20). Peace promotes joy. Once again the nativity angels remind us of this relationship. *Joy* is the watchword of the Christmas season, but then so is *peace*. Peace and celebration keep the same place, spreading a common wonder over each adoring soul.

In the spring of 1945, Mrs. Pace called us, the students of Woodrow Wilson Grade School, into our school's tiny auditorium, and told us that the war with Germany was over. The European Theater of War was at last silent. We could hear people outside the school lighting firecrackers. (I still, years later, wonder where they got them, for all such things were unobtainable during the war.) I could not even imagine how far Berlin was from our little center of life in Garfield County, Oklahoma, but the announcement of peace was indeed a pronouncement of joy worldwide. Even in my little hometown it brought dancing in the streets.

Peace brings joy!

By odd coincidence, that very year was the year that I came to faith in Christ. I learned, even as a nine-year-old child, that peace had another definition that quieted the human heart on a different level. The final year of the war had been a terrible ordeal for me. I had suffered much that year as I watched my mother agonizing over the news from the u.s. fronts. My older sisters were all married to servicemen. (One of them, sadly, died in occupied Japan around the time of my conversion.) So when Jesus entered my life, peace calmed my childish heart, and joy—a welcome reprieve after so many joyless years—was mine and has remained mine to this day.

Questions for Personal Reflection

1. Based on your joy, how peaceful are you on the inside?

2. What interferes with your expressions of joy?

Day 6: Hezekiah—Destroying Idols for Peace
Read 2 Kings 18:1–5

Hezekiah came to the throne of Judah when he was twenty-five years old. He lived and reigned in troubled times. All around him great empires feuded, and powerful armies marched. In his fourth year, Shalmanezer of Assyria came to the gates of Samaria, the northern kingdom, and laid siege to it. Israel fell to the Assyrians during Hezekiah's sixth year of reign. In his fourteenth year, Sennacherib came against the fortified cities of his kingdom (except Jerusalem) and captured them all. An era of war spread in every direction. For a while it looked as though Sennacherib would take Jerusalem too. Hezekiah went to the Lord in entreaty, and God heard his prayer. Isaiah sent word to the king that he needn't worry about Sennacherib, for God had heard his prayer and would take care of the Assyrians in his own way.

> *That night the angel of the LORD went out and put to death a hundred and eighty-five thousand men in the Assyrian camp. When the people got up the next morning—there were all the dead bodies! So Sennacherib king of Assyria broke camp and withdrew. He returned to Nineveh and ... one day, while he was worshiping in the temple of his god Nisroch, his sons ... cut him down with the sword.... And Esarhaddon his son succeeded him as king.*
> —2 Kings 19:35–37

Herodotus, a Greek historian, tells of the same event, suggesting that a plague obliterated Assyria. But whatever method the death angel used, Hezekiah's kingdom was spared.

In that same span of time, Hezekiah became ill and was near death. He cried out to God for healing. God heard his petition and extended his life another fifteen years (2 Kings 20:6). Hezekiah was a great leader who followed God and, in spite of a reign completely dominated by foreign wars, he walked with God. Under his leadership Jerusalem avoided siege and knew peace.

Hezekiah's peace was due to a life committed to God. "He did what was right in the eyes of the LORD, just as his father David had done. He removed the high places, smashed the sacred stones and cut down the Asherah poles. He broke into pieces the bronze snake Moses had made, for up to that time the Israelites had been burning incense to it" (2 Kings 18:3–4).

Peace comes when we have a single focus on God. Hezekiah destroyed the nation's idolatry. When there were no more false gods, they were able to give their adoration to Jehovah alone. This king knew that single focus in adoration always results in peace.

Have you ever been torn between loving God and your idols? In pursuing secondary affections, you can lose both your single focus on worship and your peace. Remember anything more important than God to you, *is* god to you. Idols always demand the honor and affection that should be given to God alone. Tear down those high places, and the God of Hezekiah will walk in peace through your life.

Questions for Personal Reflection

1. Hezekiah's peace was the result of his life being committed to God. Where does your peace come from?

2. What are some of the things we think will bring us peace but can't?

Day 7: Group Discussion

The following questions should take about forty-five minutes to answer and discuss. Each member should answer the first question, leaving the remaining questions open-ended. Everyone need not answer, but be sure all members participate.

1.   *What are the main things that interfere with your time alone with God?*

2.   *Even when we are too busy to pray, Jesus intercedes for us. What does this reveal about God's love for us?*

3.   *How can we introduce peace to our tumultuous world?*

4.   *Why is our personal peace a prerequisite for sharing God's peace with others?*

5. *How can we become authentically peaceful in the ways that we deal with people in situations we face?*

6. *Real peace is the result of a life committed to God. How can we apply this principle to the turmoil in our lives? How can we effectively share this lesson with others who are living in turmoil?*

Week 3: Peace—The Evidence of Confidence

Memory Passage for the Week: 2 Timothy 1:12

Day 1: Peace—The Evidence of Confidence

We have God's Son in our lives. He will calm our stormy situations and give us the confidence of his presence. Mark 4:35–41.

Day 2: The Purpose of God in My Life

God's purpose for our lives always begins in our willingness to practice what we preach. Job 4:1–6.

Day 3: My Relationship with Christ

God will not leave us half-grown in our relationship with Christ. He spent the blood of his Son to purchase our salvation, and is committed to our growth. Philippians 1:3–6.

Day 4: My Service to Others

We are called to preach peace to those who have the power to create it. Philemon 17–21.

Day 5: My Personal Worship

Peace is a state of inner confidence that derives from our love for God. Such indwelling peace should be the basis of our personal worship. Isaiah 36:4–7.

Day 6: A Character Study on Thomas

John 20:19–29

Day 7: Group Discussion

Day 1: Peace—The Evidence of Confidence

Read Mark 4:35—41

Perhaps the most amazing question Jesus ever asked his disciples was, "Why are you so afraid?" (Mark 4:40). One would think his disciples had every right to their fear. After all, their ship was sinking! Wouldn't anyone be afraid in such circumstances?

Still, "Why are you so afraid?" has all kinds of implied answers, all of which are further questions.

"Is God real?"

"Has God no power?"

"Are you not our Lord?"

But these questions are a result of peacelessness. While the threat of drowning understandably inspires anxiety, a better question to ask is, "Would God allow his Son to drown when he has so much for him to accomplish?"

Can it be that most of our lives are lived without this recognition? Doesn't God have much for us to accomplish? Should not our own security in troubled times come in remembering this? We have God's living Son on board in our lives. Therefore, we may have confidence that in our own stormy situations he will calm the turbulence and give us the confidence of his presence. Then, once our storms are all at rest, like his disciples we may remark, "What manner of man is this Jesus that even our private tempests are subject to his calm?"

Questions for Personal Reflection

1. What makes you afraid?

2. How does God respond when you are scared?

Day 2: The Purpose of God in My Life
Read Job 4:1–6

If there is a hypocrisy in our Christian practice of discipleship, it may well lie in the area of personal peace. Like Job it may be that we preach peace more often than we actually live it out. One of the greatest secular philosophers of our time refused to become a Christian because there was, he felt, something "warlike" in the way Christians went about preaching peace. Christians are always making new converts with the appeal: "Come to Christ and find peace." The truth, according to this philosopher, is that Christians are terribly fierce—even peaceless—in maintaining their individual viewpoints.

The continuing proliferation of denominations is evidence that peace is not easy to achieve. Christians have been known to resort to holy war over the minutest differences in interpretation of Scripture. And of course, many churches and families have divided over such doctrinal quarrels.

Surely it is important to fight for those cardinal doctrines that define us, but what about those highly individual viewpoints that isolate Christians into camps over doctrine that is less significant? Should we abandon our peace over every issue of difference?

Eliphaz reminded Job that he had long taught that the path to peace was dependent on the ability to trust God in hard times. Eliphaz called Job to practice what he preached. It was time for Job to demonstrate the life of confident peace he had insisted that others display.

Questions for Personal Reflection

1. What keeps you from exhibiting the peace you know God provides?

2. What happens when Christians argue over insignificant doctrinal issues?

Day 3: My Relationship with Christ
Read Philippians 1:3—6

The initial joy we embrace upon discovering Christ sometimes seems absent when we face times of crisis. This is true for all believers, but can ring especially true if we are new in our faith. Crises may also prompt feelings of abandonment by God, which steal our peace and rob us of confidence.

But God makes it clear that we are to remember that his promises always remain in place, even during our seasons of doubt. "He who began a good work in you" (Philippians 1:6) will not walk off and leave the job he started. He will complete it, and complete it, and complete it. He will perform his finishing work right up until the time Jesus comes again.

He who saved us will not let us languish in some half-formed discipleship. God, having spent the blood of his Son to purchase our salvation, is committed to our growth. He longs to see in every new Christian what every good mother wants to see in her babies: growth.

A good mother wants her babies to grow. She—like our loving heavenly Father—will love those babies regardless, but she longs to see them come to maturity as responsible adults. I know a mother whose second son was born cerebrally impaired. Unlike her first son, who went on to maturity and became a successful businessman, her second son remained dependent all his life. He was never able to feed himself, and he never outgrew diapers. She gave equal amounts of love to both sons, yet was never rewarded by seeing any maturity in her second. She experienced the child's love in other ways that brought her joy, but she never knew the joy of watching him grow up.

God longs for us to grow up. He wants our confidence in his forming our maturity to produce in us a life of peace.

Questions for Personal Reflection

1. What are you doing to grow spiritually?

2. What interferes with your desire to grow spiritually?

Day 4: My Service to Others

Read Philemon 17–21

Paul declared to Philemon his confidence that Philemon would forgive his renegade slave, Onesimus. The apostle believed that his own inner turmoil, as well as that of Onesimus, would be rewarded by peace when Philemon forgave his slave.

We do not know the exact outcome of this story, but even as we read this, the shortest of all Paul's letters, we can't help but feel that Philemon did indeed forgive and reinstate the runaway slave because of the confident tone of Paul's plea. Confidence is the grand porch before God's holy mansion of peace. Paul likely could not serve those to whom God had called him until Philemon lived up to his confident expectation. Only then would peace come to the heart of all concerned.

It is a good thing to desire to live up to the confident expectation of other believers. Others count on us. They believe in us. If we knew all that God expected of us over a lifetime, we would stagger about with feelings of failure. But we do know what others expect of us. Treating them as we want to be treated goes a long way in pleasing God.

Place this longing to help others in the center of your own life. The good things they expect of you can be done. Then you will find it easier to serve, for it is hard to serve others when your own life is in turmoil. There is only one way to return to a life of joyous service: surrender the turmoil, embrace the peace of Christ, and move confidently into the ministry you served before your life became captive to peacelessness.

Questions for Personal Reflection

1. What do other believers expect of you?

2. What do you expect of other believers?

Day 5: My Personal Worship

Read Isaiah 36:4–7

Sennacherib's field commander—an Assyrian pagan—sent a message to Hezekiah reminding him that he had falsely put his trust in military alliances when he should have put his trust in God. And the real rebuke was that God used a pagan to remind a believer of his source of peace.

Imagine a beggar approaching the front door of a suburban house. He intends to ask for alms, but when he meets the woman of the house, she reprimands him for his unkempt appearance, lazy lifestyle, and poverty. She slams the door in his face, leaving him feeling dejected from the stabbing force of her sharp tongue.

The beggar then walks around to the rear of her house and knocks on the back door. When the same woman opens the door, the poor beggar remarks, "Oh, please forgive me. I came to this door hoping that the angry woman I met at the front of the house might have a sister at the back door who would be kinder and more like our dear Lord Jesus."

At this, the woman feels the sting of his truth. Peacelessness often erupts in anger. If this is true in your life, claim your confidence in grace and let peace guide you into better worship.

If God could use a pagan general to rebuke a Jewish king, perhaps we ought to seek his counsel in the ordering remarks that others give us all through life. Peace is a matter of getting into the counseling room of our own hearts where God dwells. There is enough peace in that small counseling room to serve us for a lifetime. This field commander is proof that God may use someone we least expect to point out where that room is and to ask us why we did not go there to find peace at the beginning of our troubles.

Questions for Personal Reflection

1. What does your anger reveal about your spiritual state?

2. How can you keep your peacefulness in spite of your inclination to be angry?

Day 6: Thomas—The Abandonment of Cynicism

Read John 20:19–29

Cynicism is the destroyer of peace. Cynicism is doubt, but with fangs. The more aggressive and evangelistic we become about our doubts, the more peaceless we become. Thomas was not there when Jesus first appeared to the disciples after the resurrection (John 20:24). What a pity! The rest of the disciples were "overjoyed when they saw the Lord" (v. 20).

But Thomas had no joy.

While his friends were overcome with elation, Thomas lived in grumbling doubt; his cynicism brooded like a dark serpent over a nest of eggs. The apostles' excitement at having seen the Lord alive again only added more shadows to Thomas's dark mood. Their joy nettled this poor doubter. He became angry and scathed them for their credulity: "Unless I see the nail marks in his hands and put my fingers where the nails were, and put my hand into his side, I will not believe it" (v. 25).

So the other disciples lived in joy. Their joy gave them peace. But no peace for Thomas! No, he elected to be a man at war with himself. Unnecessarily he lived through a grudge-filled week. He was downcast, and he muttered about the foolish gullibility of his superstitious companions. Hate! Dark anger! A futile, hostile mind-set! These were the thorns that grew from Thomas's cynicism.

When the week was over and Jesus came back to the disciples, this time Thomas was there. Jesus said, "Put your finger here; see my hands.

Reach out your hand and put it into my side. Stop doubting and believe" (v. 27).

Then the joy arrived! Cynicism died. Dark moods fled before the sunlight, and peace came.

All of us have doubts from time to time, but let me ask, have doubt and peace ever occupied joint thrones in your life? Your answer will most certainly be no. Doubt and peace cannot rule together. The presence of either one is so odious to the other that one of them must flee. When cynicism is gone, peace may hold sway in our lives, but *only* then. No wonder the apostle Paul wrote: "Let the peace of Christ rule in your hearts, since as members of one body you were called to peace. And be thankful. Let the word of Christ dwell in you richly as you teach and admonish one another with all wisdom, and as you sing psalms, hymns and spiritual songs with gratitude in your hearts to God" (Colossians 3:15–16).

Thomas could only sing when peace had come to reign in his heart. So it is in our lives as well. Cynicism destroys peace and sets discord into our music. Peace clears the floor of our dull routines to make a dancing place for joy.

Questions for Personal Reflection

1. Are you peaceful or cynical? Why?

2. How can you allow God's Spirit to replace your cynicism with his peace?

Day 7: Group Discussion

The following questions should take about forty-five minutes to answer and discuss. Each member should answer the first question, leaving the remaining questions open-ended. Everyone need not answer, but be sure all members participate.

1. *What are those things that cause us to fear the present? What causes us to fear the future?*

2. *Is it easier to talk about peace or to live in peace? Why?*

3.   *What are some of the things you can do to grow deeper in your knowledge of God's Word?*

4.   *What is the role of believers in the spiritual growth of other believers?*

5.   *What is the effect of anger in the lives of believers?*

6.   *What does cynicism do to the witness of believers? How can we prevent being cynical?*

Week 4: Peace—Accepting a Higher Will

Memory Passage for the Week: Deuteronomy 6:4–6

Day 1: Peace—Accepting a Higher Will

No believer is ever able to find peace by posing as a follower of God while remaining dedicated to his own will. John 21:18–23.

Day 2: The Purpose of God in My Life

Desiring to do the will of God is the way to peace. Psalm 40:8.

Day 3: My Relationship with Christ

Christ's love is available to all, and God's peace is available to all. Our prejudices must be put aside. Acts 10:9–16.

Day 4: My Service to Others

Paul was able to minister to others once the turmoil was gone from his own heart and life. Galatians 1:10–12.

Day 5: My Personal Worship

When our worship is reserved for Christ alone, we will live and walk in an atmosphere of peace. Acts 9:1–6.

Day 6: A Character Study on Luke

Luke 1:1–4; Acts 1:1–3

Day 7: Group Discussion

Day 1: Peace—Accepting a Higher Will
Read John 21:18–23

Peter managed to "fish his way back" from the resurrection hubbub that surrounded Jerusalem. Christ had come back from the dead, but his appearances were infrequent and unpredictable. At the Galilean appearance, Jesus forced Peter to face his unresolved guilt over his Maundy Thursday denials. The turbulence in Peter was called to gain peace in the only way it can be acquired—through the abandonment of his private agenda (this would obviously include his attempt to return to fishing) and the acceptance of a higher will for his life.

No believer is ever able to find peace by posing as a follower of God while remaining dedicated to his own will. When the will of God is accepted, then real peace becomes possible. Until then our attempt to serve God while having our own way results in inner turmoil and peacelessness.

R. A. Torrey, a famous evangelist, confessed that he tried for years to have his own way with how he would use his life. All the while his mother remained in prayer that he would surrender his life to God. Finally, he hit rock bottom and found himself in a lonely hotel room, toying with suicide. Then he remembered some maternal advice he had once received—that in his darkest hour, he should call on the name of his mother's God. Torrey confessed he did not even use the word *Jesus* as he called on the name of God. But even by using the odd nomenclature of "his mother's God," he found himself redeemed. Peace was his at once. All his futile plans for his own life were immediately supplanted by a higher will.

Questions for Personal Reflection

1. How do you prevent becoming an imposter rather than an authentic follower of God?

2. How have your personal plans for your life been altered by God's plans for your life?

Day 2: The Purpose of God in My Life
Read Psalm 40:8

"I desire to do your will, O my God; your law is within my heart" (Psalm 40:8).

This desire to discover peace is fundamental to all. We arrive at this desire by doing the following five things:

P ... Pray and seek the Father's plan for your life,
Abandoning all things that lead to strife.

E ... Engage your heart in sweet relinquishment
Of all that selfishness alone invents.

A ... Abandon ambitions we have known,
And cling to God's purpose as your own.

C ... Consecrate yourself to walk in grace,
Accept God's sovereign path and pace.

E ... Endow your mind with focus, then fill
Up with God's sweet higher will.

This acrostic is the psalmist's recipe for peace. Make it yours and you will find that not only will turmoil be gone, but meaning will flood your life. It will all happen because you will have supplanted your selfish agenda with the noblest of desires.

Questions for Personal Reflection

1. What has been your recipe for peace?

2. What recipes for peace do other people use?

Day 3: My Relationship with Christ

Read Acts 10:9–16

Peter had a vision that taught him to abandon prejudice and find the simpler peace that Jewish Christians knew was available on a much wider basis. How is this vision to be interpreted? What do the various parts of it mean? Let us examine it piece by piece.

Peter was hungry, and the vision came to him while he was waiting for his dinner to be prepared. Our appetites are so ordinary and so customary, and yet eating and drinking takes up much of our days. God spoke to Peter just before dinner. Could it be that through something as trivial as food, God wants to speak to us about how to widen our spiritual hunger? As Jesus said to the disciples in John 4:32: "I have food to eat that you know nothing about." God had such delicious meat to offer if only Peter could get past some of his old biases. He might then have been able to sate himself on a much more universal dream of God.

"Get up, Peter. Kill and eat," cried the voice in the vision (Acts 10:13). And Peter might have responded to the voice had the things in the sheet been on his kosher list. But they were not, and he protested the order.

"I don't eat stuff that is not pure and clean!" Peter protested.

"Never call what I have cleansed, unclean," said the voice.

The vision was repeated three times, just in case Peter needed the time to think it all through. At the completion of the vision, Peter could see that he needed to step over some prejudicial notions if the gospel was ever to make its way among the Gentiles.

Peter accepted God's higher will, and, as a result, peace came not only to Peter but to the entire house of Cornelius as well. This should not surprise us. Peace always comes from accepting a higher will than our own.

Questions for Personal Reflection

1. What are those things for which you are hungry? How many of them have spiritual significance?

2. What prejudices do you need to step over in order to share Christ with those who have never known him?

Day 4: My Service to Others

Read Galatians 1:10–12

Consider the verses above and ask yourself, what did Paul's acceptance of a higher will really mean in relationship to his service to others? It meant this: Paul could really minister to others once the turmoil from his own heart and life was gone. Notice his testimony in the verses that follow:

> *For you have heard of my previous way of life in Judaism, how intensely I persecuted the church of God and tried to destroy it. I was advancing in Judaism beyond many Jews of my own age and was extremely zealous for the traditions of my fathers. But when God, who set me apart from birth and called me by his grace, was pleased to reveal his Son in me so that I might preach him among the Gentiles, I did not consult any man, nor did I go up to Jerusalem to see those who were apostles before I was, but I went immediately into Arabia and later returned to Damascus.... And they praised God because of me.*
> —Galatians 1:13–24

The voice that spoke to Paul on the Damascus road said to him, "It is hard for you to kick against the goads" (Acts 26:14). The implication was that Paul's conscience was far from settled in his persecution of

Christians. Great ideas gain acceptance in stubborn hearts very slowly. Peace comes equally slowly. In fact, peace usually gets a little blood on its tranquility before troubled hearts reach acceptance.

Peace is ours to give when we have accepted life by a higher will. Peace, in Paul's own confession, sets us free to minister in ways we have never imagined.

Questions for Personal Reflection

1. To what significant purpose is God calling you?

2. How have your past experiences equipped you for this work?

Day 5: My Personal Worship

Read Acts 9:1–6

Paul met Jesus on the Damascus road and was forever changed. As a result, the world was never the same. Paul was once, by his own testimony, a devout Jew, and there can be no question about his later devotion to Christianity. But one question that arises is, how did the nature of Paul's personal worship change after he met Jesus?

Paul loved God and must have spent himself in trying to please God. He loved Judaism with all its attributes and traditions. He must have surveyed the temple with pride, adored the Pentateuch, and kept the feasts and observances in utter sincerity. So fervent was he, in fact, that he gave himself to destroy Christianity; he believed God wanted it stamped out so that Judaism would be unrivaled by a new "ism" of any sort.

Then he met Jesus!

Suddenly, his adoration took on a very personal tone. From the very beginning he must have realized that here was a new way of worship that focused on the reality that Christ was the fountain of all truth. Then he worshiped, and the result of that worship was a sweet peace that centered on Jesus.

There can be no doubt that Christianity is a relationship religion. We worship truth only in so far as that truth adheres to the person of Christ and his teaching. We are born again because we become related to Christ. We sing, "What a Friend We Have in Jesus," not "What a friend we have in doctrines." None of us runs off to worship just to exalt six rules of peace, eight principles of grace, or even the Ten Commandments. We are concerned with dogma only because Jesus has called us to God's truth, righteous living, and clear thinking. But our worship is reserved for Christ alone. When it is in place, we will live and walk in an atmosphere of peace.

Questions for Personal Reflection

1. We know what God saved us from, but what did he save you to do?

2. How is this purpose being lived out in your daily life?

Day 6: Luke—Finding God's Purpose for Your Life
Read Luke 1:1–4; Acts 1:1–3

Luke wrote two of the most important documents of the New Testament—his Gospel and the book of Acts. But in spite of this, we don't know very much about him. It is too bad, for without Luke's writing we would lose much of our good information about Christ. Many of the parables would be lost without this faithful biographer. The particular birth narratives of Jesus recorded by Luke are completely missing from all of the other Gospels. In short, Luke was an obedient chronologist of the life of Christ, and he blessed all the world while he still managed to remain largely anonymous. He included himself in the famous "we" passages of the book of Acts, but even there, he passed on no hint of his involvement or exactly how he served with the apostle Paul.

The introductions to Luke and Acts, however, do inform us that many were writing about Christ after the Ascension, and that we certainly do not have all the books that were written. In fact, another biblical writer, John, went on to say that Jesus was far more than the summation of all who were writing about him. John testified at the end of his Gospel: "Jesus did many other things as well. If every one of them were written down, I suppose that not even the whole world would have room for the books that would be written" (John 21:25). Luke knew this, too, and so he introduced his Gospel by saying:

Many have undertaken to draw up an account of the things that have been fulfilled among us, just as they were handed down to us by those who were from the first eyewitnesses and servants of the word. Therefore, since I myself have carefully investigated everything from the beginning, it seemed good also to me to write an orderly account for you, most excellent Theophilus, so that you may know the certainty of the things you have been taught.

—Luke 1:1–4

With such a humble beginning, Luke the physician—sometimes called the Beloved Physician—started his incredible biography. His account has a near-casual and delightful manner—the tone of a tale written by a man of peace. How did he arrive at such deportment? Though modest and self-effacing, it seems Luke was confident about why he was in the world. People who know what God has called them to do know the peace that results from the certainty that you have obeyed God's will. Luke, even in saying nothing about himself, told us all we need to know to live in peace and publish it—for his whole life was dedicated to publishing that peace in a peaceless world.

Questions for Personal Reflection

1. Luke told the story of Jesus' earthly beginning. What does that story say to you about who Jesus was and is?

2. How can this truth of Scripture become something that motivates you to share Jesus like never before?

Day 7: Group Discussion

The following questions should take about forty-five minutes to answer and discuss. Each member should answer the first question, leaving the remaining questions open-ended. Everyone need not answer, but be sure all members participate.

1. *What does an authentic follower of God look like?*

2. *How can believers experience real peace in today's world?*

3.   *What are some of the barriers to our sharing Christ with others?*

4.   *Christ's freedom releases us for God's purposes. What might God accomplish through you and your church?*

5. How does knowing God redefine our basic truths? How do those truths affect other areas of our lives?

6. The biblical writers were so passionate about their faith that they couldn't stop talking about God. Are you that passionate about your relationship with God? If not, why not? If so, what happened to make you that passionate?

Week 5: Peace—The Companionship of Christ

Memory Passage for the Week: 1 John 1:7

Day 1: Peace—The Companionship of Christ

Jesus walks alongside us; and his Word is part of the recipe for finding peace in him. Luke 24:13–16, 30–35.

Day 2: The Purpose of God in My Life

Immanuel means "God with us." Immanuel, or Christ, is God's grand promise to us. Peace is the grand by-product. Isaiah 7:14.

Day 3: My Relationship with Christ

We are to walk with Christ just as we received Christ—by faith. Peace derives from our faith in his continual companionship. Colossians 2:6–7.

Day 4: My Service to Others

Service to others can be fraught with stress, for people can bring stress to our lives. But in this ministry of life to others, Christ himself is the foundation of our peace. Micah 5:4–5.

Day 5: My Personal Worship

Peace is not a result of *where* we worship; it is an achievement of the simple fact that we worship and have union with Christ. Haggai 2:9.

Day 6: The Parable of the Rich Man and the Beggar

Luke 16:19–31 (TLB)

Day 7: Group Discussion

Day 1: Peace—The Companionship of Christ
Read Luke 24:13–16, 30–35

In 1954 Theodore Steinway was given an honorary degree by Oberlin College. At the time, Steinway Pianos had made and sold 342,000 pianos. Putting the mathematics to that many pianos, you have to multiply 342,000 by 243 strings in each instrument. And then more mathematics: within each piano those strings exerted 40,000 pounds of pressure. The stress within all 342,000 pianos would be that number multiplied by a factor of 40,000 pounds. In other words, Steinway Pianos was filling the world with tension—so to speak.

Yet Theodore Steinway was not given an honorary degree for creating tension. There are no degrees given for that. He was given a degree for creating harmony and beautiful music across the globe. And Theodore Steinway and his predecessors had created great harmony and music out of tension.

Jesus walked along the road to Emmaus with two people who were staggering beneath an immense load of bereavement and grief. Their hearts were heavy. There was enough tension within each of them to make even a Steinway piano feel unstressed. Yet their testimony upon reflection was, "Did not our heart burn within us while He talked with us on the road, and while He opened the Scriptures to us?" (Luke 24:32 NKJV).

Walking next to Christ, our constant companion, and using his Word to light our way, we can find a path of inner peace.

Questions for Personal Reflection

1. What creates tension in your life?

2. How do you usually deal with tension?

Day 2: The Purpose of God in My Life

Read Isaiah 7:14

"The Lord himself will give you a sign," said Isaiah. "The virgin will be with child and will give birth to a son, and will call him Immanuel" (Isaiah 7:14). Presence is the promise, for *Immanuel* means "God with us." Peace is the promise, for God's presence is the end of turmoil.

Immanuel is the grand promise. Peace is the grand by-product.

Years ago I wrote of this promise and its resultant peace:

> *Once in every universe*
> *Some world is worry-torn*
> *And hungry for a global lullaby.*
> *O rest, poor race, and hurtle on through space—*
> *God has umbilicaled himself to straw,*
> *Laid by his thunderbolts and learned to cry.*[1]

When God got serious about peace, he came as a baby. Babies are powerful forces for peace. They come in utter dependency. Helpless, needy, unthreatening, requiring love to exist. No wonder Isaiah's sign of peace was a baby.

But Immanuel doesn't just say, "God is with us." We must couple together the word *Immanuel* with the word *Golgotha*—the place where Jesus was crucified. Then we understand the permanence of peace and the victory of peace. For these two words—*Immanuel, Golgotha*—say that God is not only with us but with us *regardless*.

Questions for Personal Reflection

1. What causes you to doubt God's presence with you?

2. How can you be reminded of God's promise to always be with you regardless of your situation in life?

Day 3: My Relationship with Christ
Read Colossians 2:6–7

An immense outline for the path of peace leaps from this passage in Colossians. Consider it:

1. Peace is a faith proposition.

Just as we have received, so are we to walk. We cannot be saved without a confident faith. Faith appropriates eternity. Faith makes us friends with God. Faith hands us the key to the safety deposit box holding all God's promises, and we are instant heirs of all that Christ will inherit (Romans 8:17).

2. Continuing in Christ is a peace proposition.

Our ongoing relationship with Christ is a peace proposition. No one can be endowed with a spirit of continual inner harmony unless they have a steadfast continuance in Christ.

3. Being rooted in Christ is faith and peace.

Being rooted involves more than just walking; it requires going deeper as a result of our desire. Faith and peace do not come spontaneously from a shallow preoccupation with religious things. Unless we desire ever-greater levels of devotion, the foundations of our peace will crumble under our own growing spiritual disinterest.

4. Thankfulness is our overflowing response to the blessings of faith and peace, and in this attitude we walk with joy. Our peace is published by our very demeanor.

In short, all is gained when we walk by the same force with which we have been saved. Peace marks our lives, and the world is transformed by the picture of grace we paint.

Questions for Personal Reflection

1. If your life is a picture of peace, what do other people think peace is?

2. How can you obtain more of God's peace?

Day 4: My Service to Others

Read Micah 5:4–5

Micah's teaching that Christ is our peace suggests these five truths. In fact Micah named for us the five virtues of Christ's peace:

1. The shepherding of Christ
2. The strength of the Lord
3. The majesty of his Name
4. Secure living
5. A ministry that extends to the end of the earth

It is Christ our Shepherd who leads.

It is Christ our Strength who empowers us.

It is Christ the Name by which we find out who we are and hallow our reasons for being in the world.

It is Christ our Security, by whose protective providence we bless each coming day and are unafraid.

It is in Christ's ministry to the ends of the earth that the church finds her one supreme purpose in the world. What a gift this is! When any church sees that this is its reason to be, then that church is indeed a place of unity and joy. But when any church forgets this, it is destined to live out an uneasy and quarrelsome lifetime. Christ has called us to be redemptive. Redemption saves the lost and prevents them from an eternity without Christ. But it also saves each individual believer from pointlessness and utter irrelevance.

Questions for Personal Reflection

1. What gives your life relevance and meaning?

2. How can you be unafraid of tomorrow? What is the role of your faith in overcoming that fear?

Day 5: My Personal Worship
Read Haggai 2:9

The glory of the house of God: what is it? Is it not the place where we go to meet with God each week? If we do not meet with him, has there been any glory? Our individual worship is greater than the house of God, still how often do we go there to feel its all-pervasive influence in our spiritual development? Peace is the real product.

When I was nine years old, I discovered the joy of corporate worship in a Pentecostal tent revival. I could tell in my very first encounter with worship that I belonged in a world where people took God so seriously they sang louder than necessary, preached longer than necessary, and held public invitations that were probably more emotional than necessary. But one thing that was clearly necessary to them was God, and God happened to me in that church—every time I went. I worshiped and even as a child was reminded that the best realities were intangible and somehow more cosmic than Oklahoma.

Ever since that time I have agreed with Micah: the best house of God is the one I'm in—at whatever moment I happen to be in one. Architecture is as insignificant as a canvas tent. When God is in the tabernacle—any tabernacle—the house of God is at its optimum. There is no such thing as an insignificant house of God. Any structure is beautiful where two or three are gathered together waiting for God to happen by. There, peace is the offering and the concord of our union with Christ.

Questions for Personal Reflection

1. When you worship, are you a spectator or a participant? Explain your response.

2. What are some of the unusual places in which you have worshiped?

Day 6: The Parable of the Rich Man and the Beggar

LUKE 16:19-31 (TLB)

"There was a certain rich man," Jesus said, "who was splendidly clothed and lived each day in mirth and luxury. One day Lazarus, a diseased beggar, was laid at his door. As he lay there longing for scraps from the rich man's table, the dogs would come and lick his open sores. Finally the beggar died and was carried by the angels to be with Abraham in the place of the righteous dead. The rich man also died and was buried, and his soul went into hell. There, in torment, he saw Lazarus in the far distance with Abraham.

"'Father Abraham,' he shouted, 'have some pity! Send Lazarus over here if only to dip the tip of his finger in water and cool my tongue, for I am in anguish in these flames.'

"But Abraham said to him, 'Son, remember that during your lifetime you had everything you wanted, and Lazarus had nothing. So now he is here being comforted and you are in anguish. And besides, there is a great chasm separating us, and anyone wanting to come to you from here is stopped at its edge; and no one over there can cross to us.'

"Then the rich man said, 'O Father Abraham, then please send him to my father's home—for I have five brothers—to warn them about this place of torment lest they come here when they die.'

"But Abraham said, 'The Scriptures have warned them again and again. Your brothers can read them anytime they want to.'

"The rich man replied, 'No, Father Abraham, they won't bother to read them. But if someone is sent to them from the dead, then they will turn from their sins.'

"But Abraham said, 'If they won't listen to Moses and the prophets, they won't listen even though someone rises from the dead.'"

Questions for Personal Reflection

1. Which character in this parable best represents you?

2. What is the danger of waiting until tomorrow to tell others about Christ?

Day 7: Group Discussion

The following questions should take about forty-five minutes to answer and discuss. Each member should answer the first question, leaving the remaining questions open-ended. Everyone need not answer, but be sure all members participate.

1. *How does tension affect the spiritual life of a believer?*

2. *How does peace come into the life of a believer?*

3. *Peace is something that we can't see, but we can see the effects of it. How do you recognize God's peace?*

4. *How do we present Christ to the world? Is the image we present consistent with the biblical image of the God of peace?*

5. *What does your worship say about who God is?*

6. *How can we make telling others about Christ something about which we are more urgent?*

Week 6: Peace—The Reign of the Holy Spirit

Memory Passage for the Week: Psalm 51:10–12

Day 1: Peace—The Reign of the Holy Spirit

Reconciliation is God's aim in this stressed-out world. He desires for us to confess Christ, receive the Holy Spirit, and enjoy peace. Acts 8:9–25.

Day 2: The Purpose of God in My Life

God intends for us to spread the gospel under the influence of the Holy Spirit. Acts 1:8.

Day 3: My Relationship with Christ

Whenever you hear God glorified, Christ exalted, and the kingdom of God proclaimed, these are evidences of the Holy Spirit. The heart moved by the Holy Spirit has life and peace. Romans 8:6–8.

Day 4: My Service to Others

The Holy Spirit is the seeker of unity. But after all things true occupy the center of our fellowship, unity is the next great agenda. Ephesians 4:3–6.

Day 5: My Personal Worship

God promises: "I will give you a new heart and put a new spirit in you" (Ezekiel 36:26). With this great renovation of spirit, we will be made ready to worship. Ezekiel 36:24–28.

Day 6: Verses for Further Reflection

Day 7: Group Discussion

Day 1: Peace—The Reign of the Holy Spirit
Read Acts 8:9–25

Simon the sorcerer offered to buy what he saw people receiving for free at the laying on of the apostles' hands—the Holy Spirit. It is obscene to try to purchase what is gained only through the submission of one's will to God's desire. Nonetheless, Simon must be credited at least for realizing he needed that peace. After all, the Holy Spirit is the greatest favor heaven ever did for earth, and to have this Spirit is the greatest of blessings. What are the wonders of the Spirit, and what is it that he does in our lives?

Come let us journey to the prophet Joel as Peter quoted him on the day the Holy Spirit arrived. Those who had been swept by wind and fire moved into the streets of Jerusalem with such mystical elation they were accused of being drunk on new wine. If only for this reason, the Spirit should be celebrated. How often do we encounter worship that owns such compelling mystery? I've often thought how wonderful it would be if current congregations were accused of being drunk on God. So often they are too dead with their own dull worship for anyone to accuse them of being filled by the inebriating God.

Into these accusations of drunken belief came the word of Joel read by Peter:

"In the last days," God says,

"I will pour out my spirit on all people.

Your sons and daughters will prophesy,

Your young men will see visions,

Your old men will dream dreams....

And everyone who calls on the name of the Lord

Will be saved.

—Acts 2:17, 21

And what is the grand legacy of all this fire and wind? Peace! Reconciliation is God's aim in this stressed-out world. The answer is never to try and de-stress things. The answer is to confess Christ, receive the Holy Spirit, and enjoy the peace.

Questions for Personal Reflection

1. How can God de-stress your days?

2. What are some areas of life in which you can encourage others to let God de-stress them?

Day 2: The Purpose of God in My Life
Read Acts 1:8

The geography of God is a map of peace. Laid out for us in Acts 1:8 is a fourfold strategy to evangelize the world. The passage speaks of the ever-widening circles of influence that the gospel hopes to attain. Like a pebble dropped in a pond, the ripples of growth sweep outward until the whole pond is affected. This is how the gospel spreads under the influence of the Holy Spirit.

The gospel, like a pin stuck in the middle of a great map, is to be preached from the center outward. Jerusalem, said Jesus, was where the Spirit would arrive; then it would sweep outward through Judea and Samaria, and finally become global. *Global* may be our word since those in the first century had not made up their minds about the nature of the universe: was the earth flat or round? But the principle is the same. The key is that the gospel starts wherever we are. The late Keith Green used to argue that missions were never a matter of "foreign" or "home." After all, everybody is a foreigner to someone. The issue is: are we acting as missionaries where we are?

"There is no use taking a lamp to Indonesia that won't burn in America," runs the cliché. But the Spirit of God takes from us this missionary delusion. Lost people are no more lost because they live across some ocean. Nor are we likely to prove to God that we have any real concern for those who live so far away if we have never wept over our own neighborhoods.

On the day he gave his Great Commission, Jesus did not say, "Since you all live here in Jerusalem, organize yourselves for mission trips. You'll find that it's easier to promote the saving of lost souls an ocean or two away." Christians are always to begin to publish peace where we are. If we won't do it here, we won't do it anywhere.

Questions for Personal Reflection

1. How does the Great Commission affect your life?

2. Why do we avoid seeking to fulfill the Great Commission with our lives?

Day 3: My Relationship with Christ
Read Romans 8:6–8

"The mind controlled by the Spirit is life and peace," affirms the apostle (Romans 8:6). Why does the mind controlled by the Spirit naturally result in peace? Because the Spirit of God champions the two things that promote peace in our lives. First, he sees the battles that cannot be won in human terms. He causes us to pace our lives so that when we get to the battles that cannot be won, we have already made peace with the outcome.

There is an old prayer promoted by Alcoholics Anonymous called the Serenity Prayer: "God grand me the serenity to accept the things I cannot change; the courage to change the things I can; and the wisdom to know the difference." It is the Holy Spirit who teaches us this wisdom.

The Spirit helps us see where it is better to accept the steel out ahead than to suffer in struggling to do what cannot be done. The Holy Spirit also promotes peace by placing responsibility for any outcome in the hands of God. When we have been obedient to the Lord in any endeavor, the outcome is not our responsibility. Our whole affair with Jesus is promoted beyond the level of "try and acquiesce." It becomes a lifestyle of "trust and celebrate." This second approach brings contentment no matter what happens. Best of all, there is no failure and no guilt. No trauma or lingering recriminations! All that is left to us is peace.

Questions for Personal Reflection

1. Transformation works from the inside out. How is God changing you on the

inside, and how do you see it on the outside?

2. What areas of your life still need more transformation?

Day 4: My Service to Others

Read Ephesians 4:3–6

Keeping the "unity of the Spirit through the bond of peace" (Ephesians 4:3) is the basis of all our service to others. Why? Well, who would want a peaceless, argumentative person to become their guide to the deeper life?

But the plea for unity in this passage is backed up by the evidence of unity throughout the entire kingdom of God. The word *unity* comes from the Latin *unus*, meaning "one." This must indeed be God's favorite number. Look at the glorious things the number one promotes in the church in Ephesians 4:3–6:

One Body—Where all believers share a common love for Christ.

One Spirit—Whose permeation of each heart produces our great commonality.

One Hope—We, all of us in his church, have no other future but God's. Jesus' second coming should be hope enough to make the church one.

One Lord—Glory of glories, the Spirit bears witness that we all know and serve one Lord.

One Faith—There is but one true universal church, which Jesus left to serve him in this world.

One Baptism—It celebrates Jesus from one confession of his lordship worldwide.

One God and Father of all.

With all this oneness, peace is as certain as sunrise. Accepting the unity of God's favorite number allows us to live in peace. Unity and peace go together.

Questions for Personal Reflection

1. How are you experiencing spiritual oneness with other believers?

2. What prevents you from having oneness with other believers?

Day 5: My Personal Worship

Ezekiel 36:24—28

When we receive God's renovation of our lives, we are ready to truly worship for the very first time. God gave us a fivefold promise to equip us to become his ambassadors of peace. Peace produces a settled inwardness, and then we are truly ready to adore him.

1. *"I will cleanse you from all your impurities and from all your idols"* (Ezekiel 36:25).

    How blessed is this promise, for when we come into Christ we finally worship the right thing, rather than worshiping idols. Idols? Yes, for anything in our lives that is more important than God is the god of our lives. Most of us have plenty of these idolatries before Jesus comes into our lives and captures our hearts. Then, after we receive Christ, we are sometimes slow to abandon them.

2. *"I will give you a new heart"* (v. 26).

    By this God is saying he will transplant our value systems and give us a new worldview. With that transplant we will have a God's-eye view of our world.

3. *"[I will] put a new spirit in you"* (v. 26).

    We will have a new energy for desiring righteousness in our lives. We will no longer be left to manage life with a whole set of inferior appetites. The Spirit will alter our wants till they are only what *God* wants for us.

4. *"I will remove from you your heart of stone and give you a heart of flesh"* (v. 26).

Compassion is the automatic by-product of our new heart transplant. God will cause us to see and care about human hurt and those who are lost.

5. *"[I will] move you to follow my decrees"* (v. 27).

There will come with God's renovation of our lives a desire for a new relationship that derives from our desire for obedience.

In short, with this great renovation, not only will the peace of God occupy our lives, but we will be made ready to worship our Lord.

Questions for Personal Reflection

1. How has God renovated your life?

2. Now that your life is renovated, what should you do with it?

Day 6: Verses for Further Reflection

Matthew 5:9: Blessed are the peacemakers, for they will be called sons of God.

Matthew 11:28: Come to me, all you who are weary and burdened, and I will give you rest.

John 16:33: I have told you these things, so that in me you may have peace. In this world you will have trouble. But take heart! I have overcome the world.

Romans 5:1: Therefore, since we have been justified through faith, we have peace with God through our Lord Jesus Christ.

Romans 8:6: The mind of sinful man is death, but the mind controlled by the Spirit is life and peace.

Ephesians 4:3: Make every effort to keep the unity of the Spirit through the bond of peace.

Philippians 4:7: And the peace of God, which transcends all understanding, will guard your hearts and your minds in Christ Jesus.

ACTS 27:27–37, 42–44

Paul's promise of survival instills the crew of the ship with peace. Paul had heard from God. And the promise was, "Not a one of you will lose a single hair from your head." This promise of peace was true—all 276 escaped death.

On the fourteenth night we were still being driven across the Adriatic Sea, when about midnight the sailors sensed they were approaching land. They took soundings and found that the water was a hundred and twenty feet deep. A short time later they took soundings again and found it was ninety feet deep. Fearing that we would be dashed against the rocks, they dropped four anchors from the stern and prayed for daylight. In an attempt to escape from the ship, the sailors let the lifeboat down into the sea, pretending they were going to lower some anchors from the bow. Then Paul said to the centurion and the soldiers, "Unless these men stay with the ship, you cannot be saved." So the soldiers cut the ropes that held the lifeboat and let it fall away.

Just before dawn Paul urged them all to eat. "For the last fourteen days," he said, "you have been in constant suspense and have gone without food—you haven't eaten anything. Now I urge you to take some food. You need it to survive. Not one of you will lose a single hair from his head." After he said this, he took some bread and gave thanks to God in front of them all. Then he broke it and began to eat. They were all encouraged and ate some food themselves. Altogether there were 276 of us on board....

The soldiers planned to kill the prisoners to prevent any of them from swimming away and escaping. But the centurion wanted to spare Paul's life and kept them from carrying out their plan. He ordered those who could swim to jump overboard first and get to land. The rest were to get there on planks or on pieces of the ship. In this way everyone reached land in safety.

Day 7: Group Discussion

The following questions should take about forty-five minutes to answer and discuss. Each member should answer the first question, leaving the remaining questions open-ended. Everyone need not answer, but be sure all members participate.

1. *Read Matthew 28:16–20. Do you feel that most believers take the Great Commission seriously?*

2. *The bookends of Scripture are pictures of paradise. What is a believer's role in sharing this message with the world?*

3.   *Why do so many people embrace the truth of God's Word but refuse to let it transform them?*

4.   *How can we become one with other believers and other churches? What is our shared purpose?*

5. *What keeps the world from embracing the spiritual makeover that we have experienced?*

6. *How can we become more effective peacemakers in our world?*

ENDNOTES

1.   *Calvin Miller,* A Symphony in Sand *(Minneapolis, MN: Bethany House,* 2001*),* 6.

PRAYER JOURNAL

Use the following pages to record both prayer requests and answers.

PRAYER JOURNAL